Restaurant Startup Business Plan for Success

Finance, Management & Marketing Leadership Strategy

By Eddie G. Sanders

ABOUT THE AUTHOR

Eddie G. Sanders is a published author of several business books & articles on personal investing and self improvement.

Eddie is a graduate of Jackson State University with a Bachelor of Science Degree in Business Administration and a graduate of Central Michigan University with a Master of Science Degree in Administration.

Eddie can be contacted by e-mail at:
egselroy1@aol.com

DEDICATION

**This book is dedicated to my wife
Ruth Sanders. The love of my life.**

Table of Contents

ACKNOWLEDGMENTS

I WOULD LIKE TO ACKNOWLEDGE ALL THE
HARD WORK OF THE MEN AND WOMEN OF THE
UNITED STATES MILITARY, WHO RISK THEIR
LIVES ON A DAILY BASIS, TO MAKE THE WORLD
A SAFER PLACE.

Disclaimer

This book was written as a guide to starting a business. As with any other high yielding action, starting a business has a certain degree of risk. This book is not meant to take the place of accounting, legal, financial or other professional advice. If advice is needed in any of these fields, you are advised to seek the services of a professional.

While the author has attempted to make the information in this book as accurate as possible, no guarantee is given as to the accuracy or currency of any individual item. Laws and procedures related to business are constantly changing.

Therefore, in no event shall Eddie Sanders, the author of this book be liable for any special, indirect, or consequential damages or any damages whatsoever in connection with the use of the information herein provided.

Chapter 1
Restaurant Business Startup

Restaurant Business Startup

Opening a new restaurant can be considered a risky business venture. However if you know the basics, you will be able to stay away from hassle and make it a profitable business within a short period of time. In other words, you need to pay special attention towards financing, planning and everything in between. Here is a list of guidelines that you can follow in order to start a restaurant business without much hassle.

First of all, you need to have a clear understanding about the supplies that are required to start a restaurant business. Here is a list of 12 of the most important supplies that you must have:

Reach in coolers.
Oven and ranges.
Basic cooking equipment.
Microwave ovens.
Convection ovens.
Fryers.
Food preparation tables.
Merchandisers.
Sinks and faucets.
Ice machines and accessories.
Transportation carts and racks.
Shelving.

If you have these 12 items, you have a good foundation for starting restaurant. Multiple sources for all of this equipment is in the business rolodex.

Restaurant Business Startup

Location Location Location

The next thing you should do is to select the ideal location to start your restaurant. It's perfectly fine to take your time and do the research before you find a place. When selecting a place, you need to pay special attention towards demographics and style of operation. Foot traffic is also a crucial factor, which can contribute towards the long term success of your restaurant. Then you need to think of parking and accessibility because the customers prefer them.

You should do a proper analysis to figure out the competition that exists in the area as well. If there are similar restaurants in the neighborhood, you should think twice before selecting it as the location. In addition, you need to consider about the proximity to other services and businesses.

The Menu

Once you select a location for your restaurant, you need to finalize your menu. This can also create a tremendous impact on the success of your business venture. When creating the restaurant menu, it is a good idea to avoid food fads. You must include some low cost food items in the menu as well. If you can include easy preparing dishes in your menu, you will be able to provide a quick service to your customers. Last but not least, you need to think about making the restaurant menu versatile.

Restaurant Business Startup

Menu engineering

Menu engineering is an interdisciplinary field of study devoted to the deliberate and strategic construction of menus. It is also commonly referred to as Menu Psychology.

Definition

In general, the term menu engineering is used within the hospitality industry (specifically in the context of restaurants), but can be applied to any industry that displays a list of product or service offerings for consumer choice. Typically the goal with menu engineering is to maximize a firm's profitability by subconsciously encouraging customers to buy what you want them to buy, and discouraging purchase of items you don't want them to buy.

Fields of study which contribute most to menu engineering include:

Psychology (perception, attention, emotion/eff ect)

Managerial Accounting (contribution margin and unit cost analysis)

Marketing and Strategy (pricing, promotion)

Graphic Design (layout, typography)

Restaurant Business Startup

Psychology of menu engineering

Perception and Attention—Visual perception is inextricably linked to how customers read a menu. Most menus are presented visually (though many restaurants verbally list daily specials), and the majority of menu engineering recommendations focus on how to increase attention by strategically arranging menu categories within the pages of the menu, and item placement within a menu category. This strategic placement of categories and items is referred to as the theory of sweet spots.

The reasoning being Sweet Spots stems from the classical effect in psychology known as the Serial position effect (aka. the rules of recency and primacy). The thought is, customers are most likely to remember the first and last things they see on a menu—hence, sweet spots on a menu should be where the customers look first and last. To date, there is no empirical evidence on the efficacy of the sweet spots on menus.

Customer perception of items offered on a menu can also be affected by subtle textual manipulations. For example, descriptive labeling of item names may produce positive effects, leading to higher customer satisfaction, and higher perceived product value. Similarly, the presence of dollar signs or other potential monetary cues may cause guests to spend less.

Restaurant Business Startup

Managerial accounting

The primary goal of menu engineering is to encourage purchase of targeted items, presumably the most profitable items, and to discourage purchase of the least profitable items. To that end, firms must first calculate the cost of each item listed on the menu. This costing exercise should extend to all items listed on the menu, and should reflect all costs incurred to produce and serve. Optimally item costs should include: food cost (including wasted product and product loss), incremental labor (e.g., cost in in-house butchering, pastry production, or prep), condiments and packaging. Only incremental costs and efforts should be included in the item cost.

The two criteria for determining which menu items should be featured on a menu have been food cost percentage and gross profit. Food cost percentage is calculated by dividing the cost of the menu item ingredients, including surrounding dish items, e.g., salad, bread and butter, condiments, etc. by the menu price. Gross profit is calculated by subtracting the menu cost as previously defined, from the menu price. Advocates of Menu Engineering believe that gross profit trumps food cost so they tend to identify menu items with the highest gross profit, items like steaks and seafood, as the items to promote.

Restaurant Business Startup

The downside of this exclusive approach is that items that are high in gross profit are typically the highest priced items on the menu and they typically are on the high end of the food cost percentage scale. This approach works fine in price inelastic markets like country clubs and fine dining white table cloth restaurants.

Managerial accounting

However, in highly competitive markets, which most restaurants reside, think Applebee's, Chili's, Olive Garden, price points are particularly critical in building customer counts. In addition, food cost cannot be ignored completely. If food cost increases, total costs must increase enough to lower the overall fixed cost percentage or the bottom line will not improve. This is not a recommended strategy for neighborhood restaurant with average checks under $15.

Those who believe that a low food cost percentage is more important than gross profit will promote the items with the lowest food cost percentage.

Restaurant Business Startup

Unfortunately, these items are typically the lowest priced items on the menu, e.g., chicken, pasta, soups. Promoting only low food cost items will likely result in lowering your average check and unless the restaurant attracts more customers, overall sales will not be optimized.

Low food cost and high gross profit are not mutually exclusive attributes of a menu item. A second approach called Cost-Margin Analysis identifies items that are both low in food cost and return a higher than average gross profit. These items referred to as Primes. This analysis works well for restaurants in highly competitive markets where customers are price-sensitive.

There is really no single method of analysis that can be used across the board on all menu items. If a menu item is a "commodity" like hamburgers, chicken tenders, fajitas, and other items found on the majority of restaurant menus, prices tend to be more moderate.

Restaurant Business Startup

Managerial accounting

If a menu item is a "specialty" and unique to a particular restaurant, and demand is high, prices can be higher than average because technically the restaurant has a "monopoly" on that item and until competitors copy them and put it on their menus, higher prices can be charged.However, no restaurant can sustain a competitive uniqueness or price advantage over their competition in the long run. Eventually competitors will try to match them.

Using Menu Engineering in restaurants or menu items where price inelasticity is present is recommended and Cost-Margin in casual neighborhood restaurants and on menu items where price points are critical in building and keeping customers should be considered. Remember, the customer determines the best price to charge, not the restaurant operator. Customers do not care about your costs; they care about what you charge.

After an item's cost and price have been determined analysis and evaluation of an item's profitability is based on the item's Contribution Margin.

Restaurant Business Startup

The contribution margin is calculated as the menu price minus the cost. Menu engineering then focuses on maximizing the contribution margin of each guest's order. Recipe costing should be updated (at least the ingredient cost portion) whenever the menu is reprinted or whenever items are re-engineered. Some simplified calculations of contribution margin include only food costs.

Restaurant staff

A restaurant's proprietor is called a restaurateur / ˌrɛstərəˈtɜːr/; like 'restaurant', this derives from the French verb restaurer, meaning "to restore". Professional cooks are called chefs, with there being various finer distinctions (e.g. sous-chef, chef de partie). Most restaurants (other than fast food restaurants and cafeterias) will have various waiting staff to serve food, beverages and alcoholic drinks, including busboys who remove used dishes and cutlery. In finer restaurants, this may include a host or hostess, a maître d'hôtel to welcome customers and to seat them, and a sommelier or wine waiter to help patrons select wines.

Restaurant Business Startup

Chef's table

A chef's table is a table located in the kitchen of a restaurant, reserved for VIPs and special guests. Patrons may be served a themed tasting menu prepared and served by the head chef. Restaurants can require a minimum party and charge a higher flat fee. Because of the demand on the kitchen's facilities, chef's tables are generally only available during off-peak times.

Restuarant Economics in the United States

As of 2006, there are approximately 215,000 full-service restaurants in the United States, accounting for $298 billion in sales, and approximately 250,000 limited-service (fast food) restaurants, accounting for $260 billion.

Restaurants employed 912,100 cooks in 2013, earning an average $9.83 per hour. The waiting staff numbered 4,438,100 in 2012, earning an average $8.84 per hour.

Restaurant Business Startup

Jiaxi Lu of the Washington Post reports in 2014 that, "Americans are spending $683.4 billion a year dining out, and they are also demanding better food quality and greater variety from restaurants to make sure their money is well spent."

Dining in restaurants has become increasingly popular, with the proportion of meals consumed outside the home in restaurants or institutions rising from 25% in 1950 to 46% in 1990. This is caused by factors such as the growing numbers of older people, who are often unable or unwilling to cook their meals at home and the growing number of single-parent households. It is also caused by the convenience that restaurants can afford people; the growth of restaurant popularity is also correlated with the growing length of the work day in the US, as well as the growing number of single parent households. Eating in restaurants has also become more popular with the growth of higher income households. At the same time, less expensive establishments such as fast food establishments can be quite inexpensive, making restaurant eating accessible to many.

Restaurant Business Startup

Regulations

In many counties, restaurants are subject to inspections by health inspectors to maintain standards for public health, such as maintaining proper hygiene and cleanliness. As part of these inspections, cooking and handling practices of ground beef are taken into account to protect against the spread of E coli poisoning.

The most common kind of violations of inspection reports are those concerning the storage of cold food at appropriate temperatures, proper sanitation of equipment, regular hand washing and proper disposal of harmful chemicals. Simple steps can be taken to improve sanitation in restaurants. As sickness is easily spread through touch, restaurants are encouraged to regularly wipe down tables, door knobs and menus.

Depending on local customs and the establishment, restaurants may or may not serve alcoholic beverages. Restaurants are often prohibited from selling alcoholic beverages without a meal by alcohol sale laws; such sale is considered to be activity for bars, which are meant to have more severe restrictions. Some restaurants are licensed to serve alcohol ("fully licensed"), and/or permit customers to "bring your own" alcohol (BYO / BYOB). In some places restaurant licenses may restrict service to beer, or wine and beer.

Restaurant Business Startup

Your Restaurant Building

Most of the people who are planning to open new restaurants wonder whether they should lease the building or purchase it. If you are starting your restaurant with a limited amount of capital, you can think of leasing the building.

Leasing can help you to save money, which can be used to design the dining area, upgrade the kitchen and promote your restaurant. However, you will have to agree to the restrictions of the landlord when you are modifying the restaurant according to your preferences.

If you want to stay away from leasing hassles you can always purchase the building. This is the recommended option available for the people who start new restaurants while keeping long term success in mind.

When looking to buy a property try to cast a wide net and look at as many properties as possible. Don't be shy about contacting a real estate agent that specializes in commercial property.

Chapter 2

HOW TO GET STARTED STEP BY STEP

How to get started step by step

Starting a business involves planning, making key financial decisions and completing a series of legal activities. These 12 easy steps can help you plan, prepare and manage your business.

Step 1: Write a Business Plan

Use these tools and resources to create a business plan. This written guide will help you map out how you will start and run your business successfully.

Step 2: Get Business Assistance and Training

Take advantage of free training and counseling services, from preparing a business plan and securing financing, to expanding or relocating a business from the Small Business Administration.

Step 3: Choose a Business Location

Get advice on how to select a customer-friendly location and comply with zoning laws.

Step 4: Finance Your Business

Find government backed loans, venture capital and research grants to help you get started.

How to get started step by step

Step 5: Determine the Legal Structure of Your Business Decide which form of ownership is best for you: sole proprietorship, partnership, Limited Liability Company (LLC), corporation, S corporation, nonprofit or cooperative.

Step 6: Register a Business Name ("Doing Business As") Register your business name with your state government.

Step 7: Get a Tax Identification Number

Learn which tax identification number you'll need to obtain from the IRS and your state revenue agency.

Step 8: Register for State and Local Taxes

Register with your state to obtain a tax identification number, workers' compensation, unemployment and disability insurance.

Step 9: Obtain Business Licenses and Permits

Get a list of federal, state and local licenses and permits required for your business.

Step 10: Understand Employer Responsibilities

Learn the legal steps you need to take to hire employees.

How to get started step by step

Step 11: Get Equipment and Supplies

Get everything together that you'll need in order to actually operate. This includes items such as a truck, chemicals, equipment, and the various business forms such as service contracts. Once you have these things together, you can start the marketing process in order to get new customers.

Step 12: Your Marketing Plan

Coming up with your overall marketing plan, and implementing that plan. When you're just starting, it is usually best to choose one or two major marketing strategies, and work on those until you're getting a steady stream of customers.

Once you've gotten good at once specific marketing avenue, then it's a good idea to move on to another one, and repeat the process. You can begin with "Zero cost marketing" and scale up once you are bringing in constant sales.

Chapter 3

How to Write A Business Plan

How to Write a Business Plan

Millions of people want to know what is the secret to making money. Most have come to the conclusion that it is to start a business. So how to start a business? The first thing you do to start is business is to create a business plan.

A business plan is a formal statement of a set of business goals, the reasons they are believed attainable, and the plan for reaching those goals. It may also contain background information about the organization or team attempting to reach those goals.

A professional business plan consists of eight parts.

1. Executive Summary

The executive summary is a very important part of your business plan. Many consider it the most important because it this part of your plan gives a summary of the current state of your business, where you want to take it and why the business plan you have made will be a success. When requesting funds to start your business, the executive summary is an chance to get the attention of a possible investor.

How to Write a Business Plan

2. Company Description

The company description part of your business plan gives a high level review of the different aspects of your business. This is like putting your elevator pitch into a brief summary that can help readers and possible investors quickly grasp the goal of your business and what will make it stand out, or what unique need it will fill.

3. Market Analysis

The market analysis part of your business plan should go into detail about your industries market and monetary potential. You should demonstrate detailed research with logical strategies for market penetration. Will you use low prices or high quality to penetrate the market?

4. Organization and Management

The Organization and Management section follows the Market Analysis. This part of the business plan will have your companies organizational structure, the type of business structure of incorporation, the ownership, management team and the qualifications of everyone holding these positions including the board of directors if necessary.

How to Write a Business Plan

5. Service or Product Line

The Service or Product Line part of your business plan gives you a chance to describe your service or product. Focus on the benefits to the customers more than what the product or service does. For example, a air conditioner makes cold air. The benefit of the product is it cools down and makes customers more comfortable whether they are driving in bumper to bumper traffic or are sick and sitting in a nursing home. Air Conditioners fill a need that could mean the difference between life and death. Use this section to state what are the most important benefits of your product or service and what need it fills.

6. Marketing and Sales

Having a proven marketing plan is essential element to the success of any business. Today online sales are dominating the marketplace. Present a strong internet marketing plan as well as social media plan. YouTube videos, Facebook Ads and Press Releases all can be part of your internet marketing plan. Passing out flyers and business cards are still an effective way to reach potential customers.

Use this part of your business plan to state your projected sales and how you came to that number. Do your research on similar companies for possible statistics on sales numbers.

How to Write a Business Plan

7. Funding Request

When you write your Funding Request section of your business plan, be sure to be detailed and have documentation of the cost of supplies, building space, transportation, overhead and promotion of your business.

8. Financial Projections

The following is a list of the important financial statements to include in your business plan packet.

Historical Financial Data

Your historical financial data would be bank statements, balance sheets and possible collateral for your loan.

Prospective Financial Data

The prospective financial data section of your business plan should show your potential growth within your industry, projecting out for at least the next five years.

You can have monthly or quarterly projections for the first year. Then project from year to year.

Include a ratio and trend analysis for all of your financial statements. Use colorful graphs to explain positive trends, as part of the financial projections section of your business plan.

How to Write a Business Plan

Appendix

The appendix should not be part of the main body of your business plan. It should only be provided on a need to know basis. Your business plan may be seen by a lot of people and you don't want certain information available to everybody. Lenders may need such information so you should have an appendix ready just in case.

The appendix would include:

Credit history (personal & business)

Resumes of key managers

Product pictures

Letters of reference

Details of market studies

Relevant magazine articles or book references

Licenses, permits or patents

Legal documents

Copies of leases

How to Write a Business Plan

Building permits

Contracts

List of business consultants, including attorney and accountant

Keep a record of who you allow to see your business plan.

Include a Private Placement Disclaimer. A Private Placement Disclaimers is a private placement memorandum (PPM) is a document focused mainly on the possible downsides of an investment.

Chapter 4

Goldmine Government Grants

How to write a Winning Grant Proposal

Goldmine of Government Grants

Government grants. Many people either don't believe government grants exist or they don't think they would ever be able to get government grant money.

First lets make one thing clear. Government grant money is **YOUR MONEY**. Government money comes from taxes paid by residents of this country. Depending on what state you live in, you are paying taxes on almost everything....Property tax for your house. Property tax on your car. Taxes on the things you purchase in the mall, or at the gas station. Taxes on your gasoline, the food you buy etc.

So get yourself in the frame of mind that you are not a charity case or too proud to ask for help, because billionaire companies like GM, Big Banks and most of Corporate America is not hesitating to get their share of **YOUR MONEY**!

There are over two thousand three hundred (2,300) Federal Government Assistance Programs. Some are loans but many are formula grants and project grants. To see all of the programs available go to:

Grants.gov

WRITING A GRANT PROPOSAL

The Basic Components of a Proposal

There are eight basic components to creating a solid proposal package:

1. The proposal summary;

2. Introduction of organization;

3. The problem statement   (or needs assessment);

4. Project objectives;

5. Project methods or design;

6. Project evaluation;

7. Future funding; and

8. The project budget.

WRITING A GRANT PROPOSAL

The Proposal Summary

The Proposal Summary is an outline of the project goals and objectives. Keep the Proposal Summary short and to the point. No more that 2 or 3 paragraphs. Put it at the beginning of the proposal.

Introduction

The Introduction portion of your grant proposal presents you and your business as a credible applicant and organization.

Highlight the accomplishments of your organization from all sources: newspaper or online articles etc. Include a biography of key members and leaders. State the goals and philosophy of the company.

The Problem Statement

The problem statement makes clear the problem you are going to solve(maybe reduce homelessness). Make sure to use facts. State who and how those affected will benefit from solving the problem. State the exact manner in how you will solve the problem.

WRITING A GRANT PROPOSAL

Project Objectives

The Project Objectives section of your grant proposal focuses on the Goals and Desired outcome.

Make sure to indentify all objectives and how you are going to reach these objectives. The more statistics you can find to support your objectives the better. Make sure to put in realistic objectives. You may be judged on how well you accomplish what you said you intended to do.

Program Methods and Design

The program methods and design section of your grant proposal is a detailed plan of action.

What resources are going to be used.

What staff is going to be needed.

System development.

Create a Flow Chart of project features.

Explain what will be achieved.

Try to produce evidence of what will be achieved.

Make a diagram of program design.

WRITING A GRANT PROPOSAL

Evaluation

There is product evaluation and process evaluation. The product evaluation deals with the result that relate to the project and how well the project has met it's objectives.

The process evaluation deals with how the project was conducted, how did it line up with the original stated plan and the overall effectiveness of the different aspects of the plan.

Evaluations can start at anytime during the project or at the project's conclusion. It is advised to submit a evaluation design at the start of a project.

 It looks better if you have collected convincing data before and during the program.

If evaluation design is not presented at the beginning that might encourage a critical review of the program design.

Future Funding

The Future Funding part of the grant proposal should have long term project planning past the grant period.

WRITING A GRANT PROPOSAL

Budget

Utilities, rental equipment, staffing, salary, food, transportation, phone bills and insurance are just some of the things to include in the budget.

A well constructed budget accounts for every penny.

For a complete guide for government grants google

catalog of federal domestic assistance. You can download a complete PDF version of the catalog.

Other sources of Government Funding

You can get General Small Business loans from the government. Go to the Small Business Administration for more information.

SBA Microloan Program

The Microloan program provides loans of up to $50,000 with the average loan being $13,000.

sba.gov

Here are a Few Current Commercial Real Estate

Grant/Loan Programs

Program Number: 10.415

Program Name: Rural Rental Housing Loans

Department: Department of Agriculture

Assistance: Grants - Direct Loans

Program Number: 10.438

Program Name: Section 538 Rural Rental

Department: Department of Agriculture

Assistance: Guaranteed Loans

Program Number: 14.191

Program Name: Multifamily Housing

Department: HUD

Assistance: Project Grants

A Few Current Commercial Real Estate Grant/Loan Programs

Program Number: 14.314

Program Name: Assisted Living Conversion

Department: HUD

Assistance: Project Grants

Program Number: 14.326

Program Name: Rental Assistance 811

Department: HUD

Assistance: Project Grants

Program Number: 14.329

Program Name: HUD Multifamily PSF Pilot

Department: HUD

Assistance: Direct Payments for Specified Use

WRITING A GRANT PROPOSAL

Recently billionaire Elon Musk was awarded 4.9 billion dollars in government subsidies. If you are hesitant to pursue government assistance, let that sink in. A billionaire who pays little in taxes was given billions of your tax dollars.

Government grants are real. Like anything else worthwhile, there is effort and qualifications that must be met to obtain them.

Chapter 5
Colossal Cash
CrowdFunding

Colossal Cash Crowdfunding

In 2015 over $34 billion dollars was raised by crowdfunding. Crowdfunding and Crowdsourcing roots began in 2005 and they help to finance or fund projects by raising money from a large number of people, usually by using the internet.

This type of fundraising or venture capital usually has 3 components. The individual or organization with a project that needs funding, groups of people who donate to the project, and a organization sets up a structure or rules to put the tow together.

These websites do charge fees. The standard fee for success is about %5. If your goal is not met there is also a fee.

Below is a list of the top Crowdfunding websites according to myself and Entrepreneur Magazine Contributor Sally Outlaw.

Colossal Cash Crowdfunding

https://www.indiegogo.com/

Started as a platform for getting movies made, now helps to raise funds any cause.

http://rockethub.com/

Started as a platform for the arts, now it helps to raise funds for business, science, social projects and education.

http://peerbackers.com/

Peerbackers focuses on raising funds for business, entrepreneurs and innovators.

https://www.kickstarter.com/

The most popular and well know n of all the crowdfunding websites. Kickstarter focuses on film, music, technology, gaming, design and the creative arts. Kickstarter only accepts projects from the United States, Canada and the United Kingdom.

Colossal Cash Crowdfunding

http://group.growvc.com/

This website is for business and technology innovation.

https://microventures.com/

Get access to angel investors. This website is for business startups.

https://angel.co/

Another website for business startups.

https://circleup.com/

Circle up is for innovative consumer companies.

https://www.patreon.com/

If you start a YouTube Channel (highly recommended) you will hear about this website frequently. This website if for creative content people.

Colossal Cash Crowdfunding

https://www.crowdrise.com/

"Raise money for any cause that inspires you."
Landing page slogan speaks for itself. #1 fundraising
website for personal causes.

https://www.gofundme.com/

This fundraising website allows for business, charity,
educatiion, emergencies, sports, medical, memorials,
animals, faith, family, newlyweds etc...

https://www.youcaring.com/

The leader in free fundraising. Over $400 million
raised.

https://fundrazr.com/

"FundRazr is laser-focused on eliminating the
guesswork of raising money online for your
campaign. Our technology and social media guidance
make telling your powerful story easy; sharing it with
the widest community simple; and collecting the
money worry-free. "

Chapter 6
Accounting
Business Basics

Accounting Business Basics

Disclaimer - This chapter is for information purposes only. If needed, seek the help of a certified public accountant or a tax attorney. One advantage of hiring a CPA is that a CPA should have the most in-depth knowledge of the current tax laws. One advantage of using a tax attorney is that an attorney has attorney-client priviledge which can be a big asset when privacy and security of your information is a priority.

Accounting is the process of recording, reporting, understanding and analyzing financial and non financial information about the economic properties like corporations and businesses. Warren Buffett refers to it as the language of business. It has been reported that 90% of businesses fail becuase of bad financial management. So it is important that you understand accounting basics.

Recording Transactions

Revenue - The income or increase in net assets that an entity has from its normal business activities. It can also be defined as sales or turnover. Other sources of revenue can be interest, royaties or other fees.

Accounting Business Basics

Expenses - Costs incurred to run your business

Assets - Resources that are owned by the company with a measurable future value.

Liabilities - What a company ownes to creditors. Loans are an example.

Equity - The degree of ownership in your business. Your equity is the difference between your assets and liabilities. It is the difference between wht you own verses what you owe.

Reporting

Income Statement

Cash Basis - You recognize revenue and expenses based on when money is exchanged.

Accrual Basis - You recognize revenue and expenses based on when the exchange is complete. Once the service is delivered. When using this method, revenue must be earned by exchanging the product or service. It ignores the cash transaction.

Balance Sheet - This helps you understand your company's liquidity and ability to meet its financial obligations.

Cash Flow Statement - This shows the consistet cash inflows and outflows of a business.

Accounting Business Basics

Understanding and Analyzing

Analysis and understanding of a financial statements is the process of determining the significance and meaning of the financial statement data so that a prediction may be made of the possibility for future earnings. Your ability to handle expenses both current and long term.

Bookkeeping Basics for Small Business

Bookkeeping is the activity or occupation of keeping categorizing and retrieving financial records of a business. Using an accounting system to generate reports used to make better financial decisions. It should be done on a monthly basis.

1. Gather source documentation.

* Invoices

* Sales

* Receipts

* Bank Statements

* Credit Card Statements

Accounting Business Basics

Important infomation needed on these documents is the date, buyer and or seller, amount and the product or service.

2. Categorizing Transactions

* Assets

* Liabilities

* Equity

* Revenue

* Expenses

3. Reconcile Transactions

It is best to use accounting software to accomplish this task. When you reconcile your transactions you are matching all of your tranactions on your bank or credit card statements to what is in our accounting software.

Accounting Business Basics

4. Creating a Financial Statement

* Balance sheet - a tatement of the assets, liabilities, and capital of your business at a paticular point in time, detailing the balance of income and expenditure over the preceding period. Assets on a balance sheet must equal liabilities plus your equities.

* Income statement - Also refered to as the profit and lost statement contains revenue and expense transactions. This informs you how profitable you are during a set time period.

* Cash flow statement - cash your recieve from your business operation, financing and investments.

Most popular business tax deductions for small businesses

Tax deduction is a reduction of income that is able to be taxed and is usually a result of expenses incurred to produce income. They can take the form of tax incentives as well as exemptions and credits.

The IRS allows you to write-off busienss expenses that are ordinary and necessary to run your business.

Accounting Business Basics

1. Startup and organization expenses. You can deduct up to $5,000 each of Startup and organizational expenses in the first year. This limit applies if your costs are $50,000 or less.

2. Office expenses, technology, and supplies.

3. Home office deduction.

4. Cell phone and cell phone service expenses.

5. Cost of goods sold.

6. All labor costs.

7. Business expenses: Mileage, Travel & Meals.

8. Business interest expense.

9. Retirement contributions.

10. Health savings contributions.

11. Self-Employment taxes

12. Pass-through tax deduction - It only applies to specific entity types and there are income limits.

Accounting Business Basics

Free Accounting Software for Business

Some of these free versions also have paid versions as well.

Waveapps.com

Wave accounting software for small business is a easy to use accounting software that can connect to your bank accounts, sync your expenses, balance your books, and get your ready for tax time.

Wave products include accounting to track your income and expenses. Invoicing to create and send professional invoices. Payments - accept credit cards and bank payments online. Payroll - Pay employees and independent contractors. Receipts scan receipts anytime, anywhere right from your phone.

Zipbooks.com

Accounting - A complete but dead-simple accounting solution.

Billing - One-time and recurring billing so you get paid fast.

Intelligence - Full suite of reports and insights to keep you on track.

Expenses - Smart and automated expense tracking.

Accounting Business Basics

SlickPie.com

Slickpie has a free starter version and currently a $39.95 a month version. The features for both are very similar. No credit card is required to sign up. Here are the features offered by SlickPie.

MagicBot - Automated receipt data entry

Send online invoices

Multi-currency

Paypal, Stripe, and Credit Card Processing

Create Quotes and Estimates

Get live bank feeds

Reconcile Bank Transactions

Add Multiple companies and users

See transaction history

Upload and attach files

Track Expenses & Sales tax

Manage bills

See financial performance reports

Set up recurring invoices

Set up late payment reminders

Accounting Business Basics

Bank-Grade security

Run your business on any device

Get full support

Paid Accounting Software Solutions

Xero

xero.com/us

Xero has a $11.00 per month program good for freelancers, sole traders and new businesses. It's features include:

Send 20 invoices and quotes

Enter 5 bills

Reconcile bank transactions

Capture bills and receipts with Hubdoc.

Xero has a $32.00 per month program good for growing small businesses. It features include:

Send invoices and quotes

Enter bills

Accounting Business Basics

Reconcile bank transactions

Capture bills and receipts with Hubdoc

Xero has a $62.00 per month program good for established businesses of all sizes. It features:

Send invoices and quotes

Enter bills

Reconcile bank transactions

Capture bills and receipts with Hubdoc

Use multiple currencies

Track projects

Claim expenses.

One of the advantages of Xero is it is easy to tailor it to your business. One of the drawbacks to Xero is that it is not widely known in the United States and thus makes it hard to get professional help if needed.

Accounting Business Basics

Quickbooks

quickbooks.intuit.com/

Quickbooks is the number one cloud based accounting software in the world. It has four primary programs.

Self-Employed $15.00 a month

Track income & expenses

Capture & organize receipts

Estimate quarterly taxes

Invoice & accept payments

Track miles

Run basic reports

Accounting Business Basics

Simple Start $25.00 a month

Track income & expenses

Capture & organize receipts

Maximize tax deductions

Invoice & accept payments

Track miles

Manage cash flow

Run general reports

Send estimates

Track sales & sales tax

Manage 1099 contractors

Plus $70.00 a month

Everything included in Simple Start and...

Manage & pay bills

Track time

Includes 5 users

Track project profitability

Track Inventory

Accounting Business Basics

Advanced $150 a month

Includes everthing in the Plus packages and...

Up to 25 users

Business analytics & insights

Batch invoices & expenses

Customize access by role

Dedicated account team

On-demand online training

Restore company data

Automate workflows

Accounting Business Basics

In conclusion:

In order to be an owner of many of today's top business franchises, it is required that you work all of the jobs in that franchise. So even if accounting is not a favorite top of yours, it is a good idea to at least have a good understanding of it.

For more indepth understanding of accounting you can visit a training website called Udemy.com. There are many courses for under $20.00 you can take. Entire course on accounting many as little as only one hour!

There are many instructors to choose from, but one with some of the most impressive accounting credentials on the Udemy website is Chris Haroun. Chris has an MBA in finance from a Ivy League school (Columbia University). He has worked for many companies including Wall Street Hedge Funds. During his career he has raised and managed over   1 billion dollars. He uses a visual presentation teaching method and has a user rating of 4.5 stars. He is just one of many qualified instructors on this training site.

Chapter 7

Business Insurance

BUSINESS INSURANCE

Consult an attorney for any and all of your business matters.

In the early 1990's an elderly woman purchased a hot cup of coffee from a McDonald's drive-thru window in Albuquerque. She spilled the coffee, and suffered 3rd degree burns. She sued Mcdonald's and won. She won 2.7 million dollars in a punitive damages victory. The verdict was appealed and settlement is estimated at somewhere in the neighborhood of $500,000 dollars. All because she spilled the coffee into her lap, while trying to add sugar and cream.

Two men in Ohio, were carpet layers. They were severely burned when a three and a half gallon container of carpet adhesive ignited, when the hot water heater it was sitting next to, was turned on. They felt the warning label on the back of the can was insufficient. So they filed a lawsuit against the adhesive manufacturers and were awarded nine million dollars.

A woman in Oklahoma, purchased a brad new Winnebago. While driving it home, she set the cruise control to 70 miles per hour. She then left the drivers seat to make some coffee or a sandwich in the back of the motor home.

BUSINESS INSURANCE

The vehicle crashed and the woman sued Winnebago for not advising her, that cruise control does not drive and steer the vehicle. She won 1.7 million dollars and the company had to rewrite their instruction manual.

Unfortunately all three outrageous lawsuits are real. If you are going to run a business, any business, you should consider protecting yourself with Professional Liability Insurance, also known as Errors and Omissions (E & 0) insurance.

This type of insurance can help to protect you from having to pay the full cost of defending yourself against a negligence lawsuit claim.

Error and Omissions can protect you against claims that are not usually covered in regular liability insurance. Those policies usually cover bodily harm, or damage to property. Error and Omissions can protect you agaist negligence, and other mental anguish like inaccurate advice, or misrepresentation. Criminal prosecution is not covered.

Errors and Ommision insurance is recommended for notaries public, real estate brokers or investors and professionals like: software engineers, lawyers, home inspectors web site delvelopers and landscape architects to name a few professions.

BUSINESS INSURANCE

The Most Common Errors and Omission Claims:

%25 Breach of Fiduciary Duty

%15 Breach of Contract

%14 Negligence

%13 Failure to Supervise

%11 Unsuitability

%10 Other

BUSINESS INSURANCE

Things you should know about or require before purchasing a Errors and Omission policy is...

* What is the limit of liability

* What is the Deductible

* Does it include FDD First Dollar Defense - which obligates the insurance company to fight a case without a deductible first.

* Do I have Tail-end coverage or Extended Reporting Coverage (insurance that lasts into retirement)

* Extended coverage for Employees

* Cyber Liability Coverage

* Department of Labor Fiduciary Coverage

* Insolvency Coverage

If you get Errors and Omission insurance, renew it the day it expires. You must be careful to avoid gaps in your coverage, or it could result in not getting your policy renewed.

BUSINESS INSURANCE

A few E & O Insurance Providers:

Insureon

Insureon states that their median Errors and Omissions Insurance policy cost about $750 a year or about $65 a month. The price of course will vary according to your business, the policy you choose and other risk factors.

insureon.com

EOforless

EOforless.com helps insurance, investment, and real estate professionals buy E & O insurance at an affordable cost in five minutes or less.

eoforless.com

BUSINESS INSURANCE

CalSurance Associates

As a leading insurance broker, CalSurance Associates, a division of Brown & Brown Program Insurance Services, Inc. has over fifty years of experience delivering comprehensive insurance products, exceptional service, and proven results to over 150,000 insured. They serve professionals nationwide and across multiple industries, including some of the largest financial firms and insurance companies in the United States.

http://www.calsurance.com/csweb/index.aspx

Better Safe Than Sorry

Insurance is one of the hidden costs of doing business. These are just a few companies and a brief overview on the topic of business insurance. Make sure to talk to an attorney or quailified insurance agent before making any decision on insurance. Protect you and your business. Many states do not require E & O insurance. But when you see the cost of some of the settlements, it's better to be safe than sorry.

Chapter 8
Selecting the Proper Business Name

Selecting a Business Name

Ask 185 people already in business how they decided upon their business name and you will get 185 different answers. Almost everybody has a story on how they chose their own business name. Even if the business is named after their family, there's usually a nice reason behind it.

When you start a company, in a sense, you are causing a new birth to begin. This new start came from an idea alone by you or your partners. Your business will have its own bank account, and a federal identification number, it's own credit accounts, it's own income stream and it's own expenses. On paper, it is another individual! Just as important as choosing a name for your own off spring, you need to spend considerable time in deciding upon your business name.

There are several reasons why a good business name is very important to your business. The 1st important reason is because it is the first identification of your brand to your customers. Customers would want to do business with someone if they didn't have a business name yet. You could look like a unprofessional amateur who is not very trustworthy.

Selecting a Business Name

Even if you name your company "Brian's Lawn Service," a business name has been established and you are indeed considered a company. Customers will therefore be more comfortable in dealing with you.

Next, a company name normally is an indication as to the product or service you offer. "Jane's Typing Service," "Hair Club for Men," "Jim-Dandy Jack-of-all-Trades," "Laurie and Steve's Laundry," "Sherry's Gift Boutique," and "Star one Publishers" are all examples of plain business names that immediately tell the customer what product you offer.

Unfortunately, many people will choose the easy approach when naming their business. They use their name, their best friend's name, their children's names or a combination of these names when naming a business. The popular hamburger-restaurant chain "Wendy's" was named after the owner's daughter.

Research however has shown us that these "cutesy" names are not the best names to use for a business. Many experts believe that it makes a company look too "mom & pop" However, this depends on the business. If your business sells something that requires this mood or theme to appeal to your market, then it's best to use this approach.

Selecting a Business Name

My favorite way to name my businesses is with catchy names that stick in people's heads after we have initially made contact. Catchy names like, "Sensible Salt," "Dirty Defenders," "Moonlighters Ink," "Printer's Friend," "Strictly Class," "Collections and Treasures," and "Starlight on Twilight" are all good examples of catchy names. Names like these relate to your product or service and can serve as a type of slogan for your business. This is a big help when marketing.

A business friend of mine owns a business called "Mint Stripe Candy." He grows and sells his own line of raw seasonings to people in the local area. At an outing for small businesses he gave out his business card. The card had a mint candy attached on the back and the slogan read: "Your business is worth a mint to us." Using this marketing concept got him noticed and remembered and brought in several large orders for his company.

Selecting a Business Name

When naming one of your children, you may not have decide upon a permanent name until after they are born. You do this because a name is sometimes associated with a type of personality. You should wait until you know or have obtained the products you will sell or service you are offering before you decide upon a business name or even go into the business itself. Your business name should give some clue as to what product or service you are selling.

A company named "Mike's Collections" normally wouldn't sell car parts and a business named "Charlie Horse" would not sell knitting supplies.

To create ideas - start looking at business names everywhere you go. Watch TV commercial and pay attention which ones catch your eye and stay in with you. Ffigure out "why" they stuck with you. Some businesses like "Dominos Pizza" stays in your mind because it is on national TV all the time. They don't count!

Look around and notice the smaller businesses. Take your time. In a short amount of time you will be able to come up with a several potential business names.

After you finally think of a few names you really like - try them out on other people and find out what they think.

Selecting a Business Name

It won't take very long until your company will have the proper name that will carry it through it's life!

Business Name HINT:

It is a good idea to avoid very long names because they can be harder to remember and cost more in display ads. American International Enterprises can be easily presented as AIE - which is easier and shorter to spell.

Also consider names like:

Bed Bath and Beyond.

Lady GA GA

Coca Cola

Peter Parker

Clark Kent

Bruce Banner

The first and second parts of the names are similar in sound or pronuciation. This makes it easy to remember.

Chapter 9

Management Leadership & Employee Hires

Management Leadership & Employee's

When starting a business it is important to have a team of people who are willing to work hard and understand their roll in the business.

Here are some of the employee's you will need.

Statistical information from the department of labor.

Food Service Managers & Responsibilities

Food service managers make sure that customers are satisfied with their dining experience. Food service managers are liable for the daily operation of restaurants or other establishments that prepare and serve food and beverages. They direct staff to make sure that customers are satisfied with their dining experience, and they manage the business to make sure that it's profitable.

Food service managers typically do the following:

* Hire, train, oversee, and sometimes fire employees.

* Order food and beverages, equipment, and supplies.

* Oversee food preparation, portion sizes, and therefore the overall presentation of food.

Management Leadership & Employee's

* Inspect supplies, equipment, and work areas.

* Make sure that employees meet health and food safety standards.

* Address complaints regarding food quality or service.

* Schedule staff hours and assign duties.

* Manage budgets and payroll records.

* Establish standards for personnel performance and customer service.

Managers coordinate activities of the kitchen and dining room staff to make sure that customers are served properly and in a timely manner. They oversee orders within the kitchen, and, if needed, they work with the chef to remedy any delays in service.

Food service managers are liable for all functions of the business associated with employees. for instance , most managers interview, hire, train, oversee, appraise, discipline, and sometimes fire employees. Managers also schedule work hours, ensuring that enough workers are present to cover each shift. During busy periods, they'll expedite service by helping to serve customers, processing payments, or cleaning tables.

Management Leadership & Employee's

Managers also arrange for cleaning and maintenance services for the equipment and facility so as to suits health and sanitary regulations. For instance , they'll arrange for trash removal, pest control, and heavy cleaning when the dining room and kitchen aren't in use.

Most managers prepare the payroll and manage employee records. They also may review or complete paperwork associated with licensing, taxes and wages, and social insurance . Although they often assign these tasks to an assistant manager or a bookkeeper, most managers are liable for the accuracy of business records.

Some managers add up the cash and charge slips and secure them in a safe place. They also may make sure ovens, grills, and other equipment are properly cleaned and secured, when the establishment is locked at the close of business.

Management Leadership & Employee's

Work Environment Food service managers

Some food service managers oversee multiple locations of a chain or franchise.

Food service managers held about 352,600 jobs in 2019. the most important employers of food service managers were as follows:

Restaurants and other eating places 49%

Self-employed workers 32

Special food services 4

Accommodation 2

Full-service restaurants (those with table service) may have a management team that has a head , one or more assistant managers, and an executive chef.

Many food service managers work long shifts, and therefore the job is usually hectic. Handling dissatisfied customers can sometimes be stressful.

Management Leadership & Employee's

Injuries and illnesses

Kitchens are usually crowded and crammed with dangerous objects, like hot ovens and slippery floors. As a result, injuries are a risk for food service managers, who spend a lot of their time helping within the kitchen. Common hazards include slips, falls, and cuts that are seldom serious. To scale back these risks, managers often wear nonslip shoes while within the kitchen.

Work Schedules

Most food service managers work full time. Managers at fine-dining and fast-food restaurants often work long shifts, and a many work more than 40 hours per week. Managers of food service facilities or cafeterias in schools, factories, or office buildings usually work traditional business hours. Managers could also be called in on short notice, including evenings, weekends, and holidays. Some managers can also manage multiple locations.

Management Leadership & Employee's

Pay

Food Service Managers

The median annual wage for food service managers was $55,320 in May 2019. The median wage is that the wage at which half the workers in an occupation earned more than that quantity and half earned less. The rock bottom 10 percent earned $33,210, and the highest 10 percent earned $93,040.

In May 2019, the median annual wages for food service managers within the top industries during which they worked were as follows:

Accommodation $64,620

Special food services $62,240

Restaurants and other eating places $52,770

With all this responsibility it is clear that the Food Service Manager is one of the most important hires you will make. If it is not you, then make sure to do your due diligence in this hire.

Management Leadership & Employee's

Food and Beverage Serving and Related Workers Responsibilities

Food and beverage serving and related workers perform a spread of customer service, food preparation, and cleaning duties in restaurants, cafeterias, and other eating and drinking establishments.

Duties

Food and beverage serving and related workers usually do the following:

* Greet customers and answer their questions on menu items and specials.

* Take food or drink orders from customers.

* Relay customers' orders to other kitchen staff.

* Prepare food and drink orders, like sandwiches, salads, and special orders.

* Accept payments and balance receipts.

* Serve food and drinks to customers at a counter, at a stand, or at a dining area table.

Management Leadership & Employee's

* Clean assigned work areas, such as tables, or counter areas.

* Replenish and stock service stations, cabinets, and dining tables.

* Set tables or prepare food trays for brand spanking new customers.

Food and beverage serving and related workers are the battlefront of customer service in restaurants, cafeterias, and other food service establishments. In most establishments, they take customers' food and drink orders and serve food and beverages.

Most work as a part of a team, helping coworkers to enhance workflow and customer service. The work titles of food and beverage servers and related workers vary with where they work and what they are doing.

Management Leadership & Employee's

The following are samples of sorts of food and beverage serving and related workers:

Combined food preparation and serving workers, including nutriment , are employed primarily by fast-food and fast-casual restaurants. They take meal & drink orders, prepare or retrieve items when ready, fill cups with beverages, and accept customers' payments. They also warm food items and make salads & sandwiches.

Counter attendants take and serve food over a counter in snack bars, cafeterias, movie theaters, and occasional shops. They fill cups with coffee, soda, and other beverages, and should prepare fountain specialties, like milkshakes and frozen dessert sundaes. Counter attendants take carryout orders from diners and wrap or place items in containers. They clean counters, prepare itemized bills, & take customers' payments.

Dining room and cafeteria attendants and bartender helpers—sometimes collectively mentioned as bus staff—help waiters, waitresses, and bartenders by cleaning and setting tables, removing dirty dishes, and keeping serving areas stocked supplies.

Management Leadership & Employee's

They also may help waiters and waitresses by bringing meals out of the kitchen, distributing dishes to diners, filling water glasses, and delivering condiments. Cafeteria attendants stock serving tables with food trays, dishes, and silverware. They often carry trays to dining tables for patrons. Bartender helpers keep bar equipment clean and glasses washed.

Food servers, nonrestaurant, serve food to guests outside of a restaurant. Some deliver room service meals in hotels or food to hospital rooms. Many act as carhops, bringing orders to guests in parked cars.

Hosts and hostesses greet customers and manage reservations and waiting lists. They'll direct customers to coatrooms, restrooms, or a lounge until their table is prepared . Hosts and hostesses provide menus after seating guests.

Management Leadership & Employee's

Work Environment for food servers

Food and beverage serving and related workers held about 5.3 million jobs in 2019. Employment within the detailed occupations that structure food and beverage serving and related workers was distributed as follows:

Fast food and counter workers 4,047,700

Dining room and cafeteria attendants and bartender helpers 488,000

Hosts and hostesses, restaurant, lounge, and occasional shop 429,700

Food servers, nonrestaurant 284,600

Food preparation and serving related workers, all other 74,100

The largest employers of food and beverage serving and related workers were as follows:

Restaurants and other eating places 74%

Special food services 5

Healthcare and supplementary benefit 5

Retail trade 4

Educational services; state, local, and personal 4

Management Leadership & Employee's

Food and beverage serving and related workers spend most of the time on their feet and sometimes carry heavy trays of food, dishes, and glassware. During busy dining periods, they're struggling to serve customers quickly and efficiently.

Injuries and Illnesses

Food preparation and serving areas in restaurants often have potential safety hazards, like hot ovens and slippery floors. Food preparation and serving related workers, all other, especially, have one among the very best rates of injuries and illnesses of all occupations. ("All other" titles represent occupations with a good range of characteristics that don't fit into any of the opposite detailed occupations.)

Common hazards include slips, cuts, and burns, but the injuries are seldom serious. To scale back these risks, workers often wear gloves, aprons, or nonslip shoes.

Management Leadership & Employee's

Work Schedules

Many food and beverage serving and related workers are employed part time. Because food service and drinking establishments typically have extended dining hours, early morning, late evening, weekend, and holidays work is common. those that add school cafeterias have more regular hours and should work only during the varsity year, usually 9 to 10 months.

Pay

Source: U.S. Bureau of Labor Statistics, Occupational Employment Statistics

The median hourly wage for food and beverage serving and related workers was $11.06 in May 2019. The very bottom 10 percent earned but $8.49, and therefore the highest 10 percent earned a average of $14.92.

Median hourly wages for food and beverage serving and related workers in May 2019 were as follows:

Food preparation and serving related workers, all other $12.01

Food servers, nonrestaurant 11.74

Dining room and cafeteria attendants and bartender helpers 11.28

Management Leadership & Employee's

Hosts and hostesses, restaurant, lounge, and occasional shop 11.10

Fast food and counter workers 10.93

In May 2019, the median hourly wages for food and beverage serving and related workers within the top industries during which they worked were as follows:

Healthcare and supplementary benefit $11.93

Retail trade 11.85

Educational services; state, local, and personal 11.80

Special food services 11.53

Restaurants and other eating places 10.73

Although some workers in these occupations earn tips, most get their earnings from hourly wages alone. Many beginning or inexperienced workers earn the federal wage ($7.25 per hour as of July 24, 2009), although many nations set minimum wages above the federal minimum.

Management Leadership & Employee's

Tipped employees earn a minimum of the federal wage ($7.25 per hour, as of July 24, 2009), which can be paid as a mixture of direct wages and tips, depending on the state. Direct wages could also be as low as $2.13 per hour, consistent with the Fair Labor Standards Act (FLSA).

Also consistent with the FLSA, tipped employees are employees who regularly receive $30 a month in tips. The Wage and Hour Division of the U.S. Department of Labor maintains an internet site listing minimum wages for tipped employees, by state, although some localities have enacted minimum wages above their state requires.

In some restaurants, workers may contribute all or some of their tips to a tip pool, which is distributed among qualifying workers. Tip pools allow workers who don't usually receive tips directly from customers, like dining room attendants, to be a part of a team and to share within the rewards permanently service.

Employers may provide meals and uniforms, but may deduct the prices from the worker's wages.

Management Leadership & Employee's

Many food & beverage serving and related workers work only part time. Due to dining hours in food service and drinking establishments, early morning, late evening, weekend, and holidays work is common. Those that work in school cafeterias have more regular hours and should work only during the educational year, usually 9 to 10 months.

In addition, business hours in restaurants leave flexible schedules that appeal to several teenagers, who can gain work experience. Compared with all other occupations, a way larger proportion of food and beverage serving and related workers are 16 to 19 years old.

Waiters, greeters and the like, can often be the first impression that a customer gets of your business. They may also be the last impression as well. Make sure to have employees that understand the old motto that "the customer is always right". Even if they are not.

No employee should be made to suffer abuse from a guest. However employees should have a mental makeup to understand that the customer is the primary source of their income, and that the happiness of the guest should be a priority.

Management Leadership & Employee's

Chefs and Head Cooks Responsibilities

Chefs and head cooks on a day to day basis oversee food preparation and other places where food is served. They oversee kitchen staff & take care of any food-related concerns.

Duties

Chefs and head cooks typically do the following:

* Check the freshness of food and ingredients.

* Oversee & direct the work of cooks and other food preparation workers.

* Develop recipes and determine the way to present the dishes.

* Plan menus and make sure to serve quality meals.

* Inspect supplies, equipment, and work areas for cleanliness and functionality.

* Hire, teach, & supervise cooks and other food preparation workers.

* Order and maintain a listing of food and supplies.

* Monitor sanitation practices and follow kitchen safety standards.

Management Leadership & Employee's

Chefs and head cooks use a lot of kitchen and cooking equipment, including step-in coolers, high-quality knives, meat slicers, and grinders. They even have access to large quantities of meats, spices, and produce. Some chefs use scheduling and buying software to assist them in their administrative tasks.

Chefs who run their own restaurant or catering business are often busy with kitchen and paperwork . Some chefs use social media to market their business by advertising new menu items or addressing customer reviews.

The following are samples of sorts of chefs and head cooks:

Executive chefs, head cooks, & chefs de cuisine usually oversee the operation of a kitchen. They direct the work of sous chefs & other cooks, who prepare most of the meals. Executive chefs even have many duties beyond the kitchen. They design the menu, review food and beverage purchases, and sometimes train cooks and other food preparation workers. Some executive chefs primarily handle administrative tasks and should spend less time within the kitchen.

Sous chefs are a kitchen's second-in-command. They supervise the restaurant's cooks, prepare meals, and report results to the top chefs. Within the absence of the top chef, sous chefs run the kitchen.

Management Leadership & Employee's

Work Environment for Chefs and Head Cooks

Chefs & head cooks held over 148,000 jobs in 2019. the most important employers of chefs and head cooks were as follows:

Restaurants and other eating places 45%

Special food services 10

Self-employed workers 10

Traveler accommodation 10

Amusement, gambling, and recreation industries 6

Chefs and head cooks work at restaurants, hotels, private households, and other food service establishments. All of the cooking and food preparation areas in these facilities must be kept clean and sanitary. Chefs and head cooks usually represent long work hours in a fast-paced environment.

Some self-employed chefs run their own restaurants or catering businesses and their work is often more stressful. For instance , outside the kitchen, they often spend many hours managing all aspects of the business to make sure that bills and salaries are paid which the business is profitable.

Management Leadership & Employee's

Injuries and Illnesses

Chefs and head cooks risk injury in kitchens, which are usually crowded and potentially dangerous. Common dangers include burns from hot equipment, falls on slippery floors, and cuts from knives & other sharp objects, but these injuries are usually not serious. To scale back the danger of harm, workers often wear long-sleeve shirts and nonslip shoes.

Work Schedules

Most chefs and head cooks work full time, including early mornings, late evenings, weekends, and holidays. Many chefs and head cooks work more than 40 hours every week .

Pay

The median annual wage for chefs and head cooks was $51,530 in May 2019. The bottom 10 percent of chefs and head cooks earned but $28,370, while chefs and head cooks in the highest 10 percent earned as much as $86,990.

Management Leadership & Employee's

In May 2019, the median annual wages for chefs and head cooks within the top industries during which they worked were as follows:

Traveler accommodation $58,250

Special food services $56,800

Amusement, gambling, and recreation industries $56,310

Restaurants and other eating places $47,980

The pay level of chefs and head cooks varies greatly by region and employer. Pay is typically highest in upscale restaurants and hotels, where many executive chefs work, also as in major metropolitan and resort areas.

If your food is not prepared correctly you could lose a customer for life. However if the food tastes great and is prepared properly, the lifetime value of a customer could be tremendous.

Having a great chef or head cook is an essential part of having a successful restaurant business. It is important to find a chef or cook who loves what they do, and truly desires to make his guest happy.

Management Leadership & Employee's

The eight steps below can assist you to start the hiring process and make sure you are compliant with key federal and state regulations.

Step 1. Obtain an Employer number (EIN)

Before hiring your first employee, you would like to get an employment number (EIN) from the U.S. tax income Service. The EIN is usually mentioned as an Employer Tax ID or as Form SS-4. The EIN is important for reporting taxes and other documents to the IRS. additionally, the EIN is important when reporting information about your employees to state agencies. Apply for EIN online or contact the IRS at 1-800-829-4933.

Step 2. Learn how to keep records for Withholding Taxes.

According to the IRS, you want to keep records of employment taxes for a minimum of four years. Keeping good records also can assist you monitor the progress of your business, prepare financial statements, identify sources of receipts, keep track of deductible expenses, prepare your tax returns, and support items reported on tax returns.

Management Leadership & Employee's

Below are three sorts of withholding taxes you would like for your business:

Federal tax Withholding

Every employee must provide an employer with a signed withholding exemption certificate (Form W-4) on or before the date of employment. The employer must then submit Form W-4 to the IRS. For specific information, read the IRS' Employer's Tax Guide.

Federal Wage and Tax Statement per annum , employers must report back to the federal wages paid and taxes withheld for every employee. This report is filed using Form W-2, wage and tax statement. Employers must complete a W-2 form for every employee who they pay a salary, wage or other compensation.

Employers must send Copy A of W-2 forms to the Social Security Administration by the proper day in February report wages and taxes of your employees for the previous civil year. Additionally, employers should send copies of W-2 forms to their employees by Jan. 31 of the year following the reporting period.

Visit SSA.gov for more information.

Management Leadership & Employee's

State Taxes

Based on the state where your employees are located, you'll be required to withhold state income taxes. Visit the state government tax page for more information.

Step 3. Employee Eligibility Verification

Federal law requires employers to verify an employee's eligibility to be employed wwithin the United States.

Within three days of hire, employers must complete Form I-9, employment eligibility verification, which needs employers to look at documents to verify the employee's citizenship or eligibility to be employed within the United States. Employers can only request documentation specified on the I-9 form.

Employers don't have to submit the I-9 form with the federal government but are required to maintain them on file for 3 years after the date of hire or one year after the date of the employee's termination, whichever is later.

Employers can use information taken from the form I-9 to electronically verify the utilization eligibility of newly hired employees by registering with E-Verify.

Management Leadership & Employee's

Visit the U.S. Immigration and Customs Enforcement agency's I-9 website ICE.gov and find more information.

Step 4. Register together with your State's New Hire Reporting Program

All employers are required to report newly hired and re-hired employees to a state directory within 20 days of their hire or rehire date.

Step 5. Obtain Workers' Compensation Insurance

All businesses with employees are required to hold workers' compensation coverage through a insurance carrier, on a self-insured basis or through their state's Workers' Compensation Insurance program.

Step 6. Post Required Notices

Employers are required to display certain posters within the workplace that inform employees of their rights and employer responsibilities under labor laws. Visit the Workplace Posters page for specific federal and state posters you will need for your business.

DOL.gov

Management Leadership & Employee's

Step 7. File Your Taxes

Generally, employers who pay wages subject to tax withholding, Social Security and Medicare taxes must file IRS Form 941, Employer's Quarterly Federal income tax return . For more information, visit IRS.gov.

New and existing employers should consult the IRS Employer's Tax Guide to know all their federal tax filing requirements.

Step 8. Get Organized and Keep Yourself Informed

Being an honest employer doesn't stop with fulfilling your various tax and reporting obligations.

Maintaining a healthy and fair workplace, providing benefits and keeping employees informed about your company's policies are key to your business' success.

Management Leadership & Employee's

Here are some additional steps you ought to take after you've hired your first employee:

Set up Recordkeeping

In addition to requirements for keeping payroll records of your employees for tax purposes, certain federal employment laws also require you to maintain records about your employees.

Websites already listed in this chapter provide more information about federal reporting requirements:

Tax Recordkeeping Guidance

Labor Recordkeeping Requirements

Occupational Safety and Health Act Compliance Employment Law Guide (employee benefits chapter) Apply Standards that Protect Employee Rights

osha.gov

Complying with standards for employee rights with regard to civil right and fair labor standards be a priority. Department of Labor's Employment Law Guide. webapps.dol.gov/elaws/elg/

Also, visit the Equal Employment Opportunity Commission and Fair Labor Standards Act.

Eeoc.gov

Chapter 10

How to Reach a Billion People for Free!

YouTube Video Marketing Overview

Million Dollar Video Marketing

When you read the title of this book you may have thought the term "Million Dollar" was hyperbole. However the beauty of video marketing is that it can be done for free, and that there really are several people who make millions of dollars just on their YouTube video's alone. Meaning that they allow ads to be placed on them and they get paid a portion of what google gets from businesses that runs the ads.

Since they are only getting a portion of what is being paid, that means if they make a million dollars, the video's actually produced multi-millions of dollars in ad revenue.

Here are a list of YouTube Millionaires as reported by Forbes magazine in the 20 December 2016 issue.

Youtube name/channel	2016 Income
1. Pewdiepie	$15 Million

Makes video's of himself playing video games and making crude comments on girls dancing.

2. Atwood	$8 Million

YouTube Video Marketing
Overview

Promotes products and tours with other Youtubers.

3. Lilly Singh $7.5 Million

Makes comedy skits mostly featuring herself talking about her parents and relationship issues.

YouTube name/channel	2016 Income
4. Smosh	$7 Million
Comedy Duo.	
5. Rosanna Pasino Nerdie Nummies	$6 Million
Baking show	
6. Markipler	$5.5 Million
Comments on Video Games.	
7. German Garmendia	$5.5 Million
Got a publishing deal from his YouTube channel	
8. Miranda Sings	$5 Million
Comedian	

YouTube Video Marketing Overview

9. Collen Ballinger $5 Million

Comedian

10. Tyler Oakley $5 Million

Makes a diary. LGBT Activist

And these are just some the the top earners. There are many more making $50,000 a month talking about movies, how to put on make up or video taping a day at an amusement park.

A Few Keys to Video Marketing Success

1. Commitment

While many of the top YouTubers are funny, they take their business seriously. One of the first things you have to understand is that there is commitment needed to be successful on YouTube.

Many of the successful YouTubers put up video's daily! One such YouTuber is Grace Randolph (Beyond the Trailer). Grace comments on movie news and movie trailers. She typically uploads 3 video's a day.

YouTube Video Marketing
Overview

2. Research

Just putting up a video will not guarantee views. You have to put in research for every video. Research if the topic is popular or trending. Research what keywords you should use in your video. Research the success of other video's. Skip the research, skip the success.

3. Popularity

There are certain topics on YouTube that are extremely popular. Star Wars, Disney, Scantily clad women, video games, comedy. Know the level of your topics popularity and try to use keyword planning to max out the highest possible level. Some educational material is extremely valuable, but not popular.

ZERO COST MARKETING OVERVIEW

This is a zero cost online marketing plan for any business, cause or idea you wish to promote. This plan will show you step by step how to use online marketing featuring YouTube and Article Marketing to get free advertising for this or any product. In addition, this report will show you how to use this zero cost marketing plan to create a passive income stream.

YouTube Video Marketing Overview

A Few Key Definitions

YouTube is a video-sharing website headquartered in San Bruno, California, United States. The service was created by three former PayPal employee in February 2005. In November 2006, it was bought by Google for 1.65 Billion dollars. According to the Huffington Post, YouTube has 1 billion active users each month. Or nearly one out of every two people on the internet.

AdSense (Google AdSense) is an advertising placement service by Google. The program is designed for website publishers who want to display targeted text, video or image advertisement on website pages and earn money when the site visitors view or click the ads.

Hyperlink is a link from a hypertext file or document to another location or file, typically activated by clicking on a highlighted word or image on the screen.

Black Hat

In search engine optimization (SEO) terminology, black hat SEO refers to the use of aggressive SEO strategies, techniques and tactics that focus only on search engines and not a human audience, and usually does not obey search engines guidelines.

YouTube Video Marketing Overview

Getting Started

You get started by opening up a YouTube account. Go to www.YouTube.com and follow the step by step instructions. Then you open up a AdSense account. The AdSense account will take about a week to open. AdSense is linked to your YouTube account and land bank account. AdSense will use your 9 digit routing number to deposit a small amount of money into your land bank account. You then have to report to AdSense the amount deposited. After the deposit is confirmed, AdSense will send you a postcard to verify your address. You must then report to AdSense the pin number locate on the postcard. Once all the verification takes place YouTube allows you to connect all of the accounts and by doing so, you can now monetize your video's and create a passive income stream.

Social Media

You should join Social Media web sites like Facebook, Google Plus, Digg, Twitter, Linkedin, Tumbler and Pinterest. Every time you upload a video. When you are finished Optimizing it, you should link it to all of your social media web sites. This creates Backlinks. A Backlink is an incoming hyperlink from one webpage to another. Google and YouTube will rank your video higher if it has a good number of Backlinks. However if you have too many, and it appears that you have created them artificially, then Google and YouTube can punish you by removing your video.

YouTube Video Marketing
Overview

As long as you are backlinking organically and not using Black Hat software or Black Hat web sites, you should be find with Google and YouTube.

Show Me the Money!

Monetization involves you allowing AdSense to place ads that run before or are placed on your videos. If the ads are clicked on, you make money. If the ads are viewed in their entirety you make money.

After you have your accounts set up, you need to gather all of the tools you will be using to create videos. You can create your videos using a standard video camera and tripod and videotape yourself. Or any other number of ways you can capture video. However for this program we are going "zero cost" so there will be no need to purchase or obtain a video camera.

Getting Free Tools to Create Your Videos

We are going to use "Screen Capture" software. Go to http://screencast-o-matic.com/home to download a free screen capture software called Screencast-o-Matic. There are two versions. The Free version allows you to videotape up to 15 minutes of content and places a watermark on all of your recordings. The pro version makes longer recordings and has edit tools and not watermark. The pro version cost $15 and year and may be worth the investment once your business begins to make a profit.

YouTube Video Marketing Overview

Then next tool you will use in creating your videos is a free copy of the office software package called Apache OpenOffice. Go to https://www.openoffice.org/download/ to download the software.

100% Copyright Free Content

Now that you have to tools to create a video, you need content. Wikipedia is an excellent source of copyright free content, you can use to create your videos. There are many keyword phrases that you can use to find material. Later on in this book you will learn how to use the Google Ad Planner to get the best keyword phrases to use in your videos.

YouTube Video Marketing
SEO – The Key to Internet Riches

Search Engine Optimization

Analytics: Video Viewership

Through out this book I am going to discuss many YouTube analytics that factor into how your video is ranked in YouTube. Once someone clicks onto your video to view it, YouTube keeps track of how many minutes it was view. Videos that are viewed from beginning to end get ranked higher base on the belief that the content is good if the viewer keeps watching it. For this reason, it is usually a good idea to keep most your videos under five minutes. It addition, this allows you to create more videos to a related topic. It is better to have twenty 3 minute videos than one 1 hour video, because it is more likely that the 3 minute videos will be watched in their entirety. Also by creating 20 videos you now have 20 possible places for AdSense to place monetized ads and thus increase your earning potential 20 times.

Tags, Keywords and Keyword Phrases

Tags, keywords and keyword phrases are the most important part of getting your YouTube video to rank on the first page of YouTube. There is an old saying..."If you commit murder, where do you hide the body, where nobody will find it? On the second page of Google".

YouTube Video Marketing
SEO – The Key to Internet Riches

Although we are working on YouTube the principle is the same. You must rank on the first page of YouTube in order for your video to get views from standard YouTube web site traffic.

Keywords are words that relate to your video. Some keywords for business are:

Business, Marketing and Start-up

Keyword Phrases for business are:

how to make money from home, internet marketing, small business grants

Tags are Keywords or Keyword Phrases that you place on your YouTube video's editing page, in order to get viewers to find your video.

Your goal is to try to rank in the top 20(land on the first page of YouTube) for every or most of the Tags in your video.

Your Video Title

The title of your video should be a keyword phrase that you want to rank for. It should also be relevant to the content in the video. When your title, tags and description are all relevant it boosts your YouTube rankings.

YouTube Video Marketing
SEO – The Key to Internet Riches

Video Description

Each video is allowed to have a description. At the top of the description box, is where you should place a clickable or hyperlink, to either your web site or another video that you wish to viewer to see. Below the link should be a description of the video that contains content that is relative to the video. One short cut you can use it to cut and paste your video script into the description.

You video description should also have the keywords you used as tags. This adds to the videos relevancy.

You should also put links in you video to your social media addresses.

Half Time Adjustments

Any tags that are ranking your video in the top 20 should be placed in the headline/title of the video to boost their rank even higher.

One software that helps save you a tremendous amount of time doing this is called Tube Buddy.

https://www.tubebuddy.com/

YouTube Video Marketing
Writing Your Script

CREATING CONTENT

You have two options for creating content. On screen video of yourself using a digital camera or phone camera. Take notes of what you will discuss.

Know your topic before you hit record.

Recording Tips:

* Use good lighting.

* Try recording near a window during the day time.

* Limit background noise as much as possible.

* Use a POWERPOINT screen capture style video.

* Create bullet points

* Use free software like jing or camstudio to record it. You can also get a free 30 day trial of camtasia from TechSmith

* www.screencast-o-matic.com is another free solution.

* Use your computer's built in microphone.

YouTube Video Marketing
Writing Your Script

* Use a usb microphone is ideal, but not required.

* if you or kids have a usb gaming headset that works as well.

* most smart phones have a mp3 recording option.

Writing Your Script

Try to use words in your script that get and hold your viewers attention. Words like... you, want, now, free, limited time, All-American, imagine and how to, are just a few of the many words that are proven to stir a viewers emotions. Viewing a few copy writing videos on YouTube should help you to chose attention grabbing words.

AIDA is an acronym used in marketing and advertising that describes a common list of events that may occur when a consumer engages with an advertisement.

- A – attention (awareness): attract the attention of the customer.
- I – interest of the customer.
- D – desire: convince customers that they want and desire the product or service and that it will satisfy their needs.
- A – action: lead customers towards taking action and/or purchasing.

YouTube Video Marketing
Writing Your Script

Using a system like this gives one a general understanding of how to target a market effectively. Moving from step to step, one loses some percent of prospects.

AIDA is a historical model, rather than representing current thinking in the methods of advertising effectiveness.

A basic rule of thumb for writing your script is that one paragraph equals about 60 seconds of talking. So if you are trying to shoot a 3 minute video you what to create a 3 paragraph document for your script. Try to use words in our script that are relevant to the title of your video.

You can also cut and paste your script into a YouTube video editor, and make your video Closed Captioned. This will increase your rankings in the YouTube search engine and it will allow more people to understand your video and increase your views.

CREATING TOPICS FOR YOUR VIDEOS

It is time to brainstorm and write down topics for your videos.

Remember you could choose a video around your own information product if you had it.

YouTube Video Marketing
Writing Your Script

Get a notepad and think of 10 to 20 FAQ about your business.

http://answers.yahoo.com

Is a good source to find out what the potiential customers of your business are interested in.

Also look at articles on ezinearticles.com and see what topics come up the most for articles related to your business.

You can also browse forums related to your business.

Take a look at information products about your target market.

When you make a video that features Frequently Asked Questions each faq could be a short 1 to 3 minute video.

Use nichesuggest.com for a list of possible keyword ideas as well as seocentro and the google keyword planner.

Brainstorm 5 to 10 additional solution oriented videos. You should cover why the solution you are offering is better and why does your product recommendation solve your customer's problem.

YouTube Video Marketing
Writing Your Script

Try to think of every advantage possible. Read other reviews of similar products or businesses or view sales pages for ideas of content for your videos.

Creating a Multipurpose Close

There are certain things that you should say in almost all of your videos:

* Thank the viewer for watching

* Ask the viewer to Thumbs up or Like your video

* Ask the viewer to subscribe to your YouTube Channel

* Ask the viewer to leave a comment

* Ask the viewer to share your video link with friends or social media

YouTube Video Marketing
Writing Your Script

YOUR CALL TO ACTION

send your website visitors to a variety of places.

* A free website through weebly.com

* A free page through squidoo.com

* A free blog through blogspot.com

Use a tracking link like www.bit.ly or www.tinyurl.com

be careful as these links can change on you.

YouTube Video Marketing
Writing Your Script

UPLOADING VIDEO

Create your account at www.youtube.com you can use a google account if you have one already created. Upload your video. Then provide your keyword rich video title. Look at other examples of videos performing well in that space. Use keywords from your niche or business and topic research write a good description with the keywords in it.

Try to include at least 2 sentences in your description. More content in your description will not hurt you. Include your website link at the beginning of the description use format http://www.yourfreelink.com encourage likes, comments, or honest feedback at the end of the description. Make a call to action in the description as well.

Chapter 11
Adapting to
Business
Challenges

Adapting to Business Challenges

"In the winter, some people freeze to death. Other people ski."
Anthony Robbins

Adapt (verb)
make (something) suitable for a new use or purpose; modify.

A pandemic. A great recession. Increased competition. There will aways be great business challenges.

Many years ago, when Jeff Bezos was in the early stages of building his Amazon Busisness Empire. Many smaller books stores began to go out of business. He was asked how he felt about their situation. He replied "there is nothing stopping them from going online."

Online's share of total retail sales has steadily been on the rise—with ecommerce penetration hitting **21.3%** in 2020, Digital Commerce 360 estimates. That's up from 15.8% in 2019 and 14.3% in 2018.

Adapting to Business Challenges

Starting an Online Business

FREE WEB HOSTING

Get a free web site. You can get a free web site at weebly.com or wix.com. Or just type "free web hosting" in a google, bing or yahoo search engine.

Free web hosting is something you can use for a varitey or reasons. However many free web hosting sites add an extention to the name of you web address that lets everyone know you are using their services. For this reason you eventually want to scale up once you start making income.

LOW COST PAID WEB HOSTING

Free is nice, but you when you need to expand your business it is best to go with a paid web hosting service. There are several that give you good value for under $10.00 a month.

1. Yahoo small business

2. Intuit.com

3. ipage.com

4. Hostgator.com

5. Godaddy.com

Adapting to Business Challenges

Yahoo small business allows for unlimited web pages and is probably the best overall value, but they require a years payment up front. Intuit allows for monthly payments.

For free ecommerce on your web site, open up a Paypal account and get the HTML code for payment buttons for free. Then put those buttons on your web site.

Step by Step basic zero cost web site traffic instructions

Step 1 zero cost internet marketing

Now that your web site is up and running you should register it with at least the top 3 search engines. 1. Google 2. Bing 3. Yahoo.

Step 2 zero cost internet marketing

Write and submit a press release. Google "free press release sites" for press release sites that will allow you to summit press releases for free. I you do not know how to write a press release go to www.fiverr.com and sub-contract the work out for only $5.00 !!!

Adapting to Business Challenges

Step 3 zero cost internet marketing

Write and submit articles to article marketing web sites like ezinearticles.com.

Step 4 zero cost internet marketing

Create and submit videos to video sharing sites like dailymotion.com or youtube.com. Make sure to include a hyperlink to your website in the description of your videos.

Step 5 zero cost internet marketing

Submit your web site to dmoz.org. This is a huge open directory that many smaller search engines go to get web sites for their database.

Adapting to Business Challenges

Create a Meal Delivery Service

According to businesswire.com the global online food delivery services market is expected to grow from $107.44 billion in 2019 and to $111.32 billion in 2020 at a growth rate of 3.61%. ... The market is then expected to grow and reach $154.34 billion in 2023 at CAGR of 11.51%.

Hello Fresh

Blue Apron

Martha Stewart and Marley Spoon

Fresh and Easy

Home Chef

These are some of the more popular home meal delivery services. Visit their websites. Maybe even order their products. Reverse engineer their success formulas and apply it to your own business.

What is their pricing strategy? How are the meals delivered? What are the most popular or best selling items?

Don't try to reinvent the wheel. The reason franchises succeed more than individuals, is that they get a success blueprint and duplicate it.

Adapting to Business Challenges

Serve food outside or start a curbside service

Of course weather plays a big part in being able to serve food outside. But if you can, making an investment in some outdoor furniture may be worth it for deversifying your business.

A easier path is having curbside pick-up. You could have a dedicated phone line just for this service. Fast customer service should be a high priority. If a person is willing to get in their car and drive to your business, they are not likely to return if they have to wait too long to get their order.

Deliver the food to their front doors.

You could have a dedicated driver you hire to make home deliveries. However now you have a employee gone for an extended period of time and have the added cost of transportation and maybe insurance.

So a better option might be to just use one of several popular delivery companies in this growing part of the food industry..

Adapting to Business Challenges

Home Delivery Service

Grubhub Inc. is an American online and mobile prepared food ordering and delivery platform that connects diners with local restaurants. The company is based in Chicago, Illinois and was founded in 2004. As of 2019, the company had 19.9 million active users and 115,000 associated restaurants across 3,200 cities and all 50 states in the United States.

DoorDash Inc. is an American food delivery service. It launched in Palo Alto, California in 2013. As of January 2020, it had the largest food delivery market share in the United States. DoorDash held its initial public offering on December 9, 2020.

Uber Eats is an American online food ordering and delivery platform launched by Uber in 2014 and based in San Francisco, California.

Users can read menus, reviews and ratings, order, and pay for food from participating restaurants using an application on the iOS or Android platforms, or through a web browser. Users are also able to tip for delivery. Payment is charged to a card on file with Uber. Meals are delivered by couriers using cars, scooters, bikes, or on foot.

Adapting to Business Challenges

Adding Merchandise to your online business

There are several types of popular merchandise that you can add to your online business. The good news is that many of the products can be handled automatically by other businesses.

Not only does selling online merchandise offer you another income stream, people wearing shirts or other products with you brand on it, helps to promote your business.

Print on demand. A print on demand is an amazing way to start a online business. Your product is only created when there is an order, so there is no need to have a large inventory and incur massive start up costs.

Amazon has a tshirt business called Merch. It does usually take months to get approved. However there is a more popular merchandise company that most social media influencers use and that's Teespring.

Adapting to Business Challenges

Teespring.com

Teespring is a leading social commerce platform for creating and selling custom products online. All products are made on demand, so there are no upfront costs or risk involved. Teespring users turn their ideas into over 50 different products instantly in the Teespring Launcher. Teespring also offers an additional service for users who have custom fulfillment and sourcing needs.

Teespring has a whole host of selling tools integrated right into users' account dashboard, including tech integrations with sites like YouTube, Twitch and Streamlabs and top brand collaborations with companies like Champion. When you get a sale they produce the product, ship it to the buyer, and send you the profit. They even take care of customer support, returns and refunds so you can spend time doing what you love, while we handle the rest.

If you would like free indepth training on making massive money on Teespring I suggest going to YouTube and viewing the YouTube channel called Wholesale Ted. This Austrailian blonde beauty has made over a million dollars selling on this platform.

Adapting to Business Challenges

Kdp.Amazon.com

Amazon kdp is a self publishing platform that helps you to reach millions of readers with a ebook or print book.

Like Teespring it is a print on demand service so if you have a book you can get started for free.

You could create a recipe book that contains a link in it to your other businesses. Having a book also helps to promote your brand an establish you as a expert in your field.

If you do not wish to write a book you can hire a ghostwriter to write your book. Freelance websites like Fivver.com and Upwork.com are a good place to start.

There are many components to creating a book that sells. While it is nice to create a passive income stream, if you are going to create a quality book be prepared to wait months to recoup your return on investment.

Adapting to Business Challenges

Kdp.Amazon.com

You can upload your book and begin making sales on Amazon in as little as three days. However Amazon holds your royalties for at least two months. If you don't already have a book made then it is likely to take another month to get all of the components created that are needed for one book.

These components are:

A completed rough draft manuscript

(for you to view and make suggestions)

A edited manuscript

(correct spelling errors once a draft is completed)

A formatted manuscript

(a manuscript that can be read on a kindle device and fits the pages on a print version)

There can be separate fees for each service.

Adapting to Business Challenges

Kdp.Amazon.com

Once you have a completed manuscript you need to do keyword research that optimizes your best chance to rank organically on Amazon. Writing a title to your book using these keywords is one of the best ways to rank your book on Amazon.

Then you need a book cover. A book description. All of this work can be done by investing in freelancers or just taking the time to learn it all yourself.

The downside can be all of the cost involved in creating just one book. The upside can be a passive income stream of book royalties not just from Amazon, but other book selling platforms for years to come.

One such example is ACX Audible Audio books. Once your book is completed they have a free option to get your book narrated if you are willing to share the royalties.

Adapting to Business Challenges

Conclusion

One of the hardest hit businesses during the 2020-2021 pandemic was the Walt Disney Company. Many felt it would be the companies doom. However Disney already had in place a popular online retail business and a growing online streaming service. These assets, loans and cutbacks helped the company to survive devastating financial loses.

A pandemic. A recession. A new competitor. We usually can't control all of the challenges that businesses face. But we do have a say in how we respond to them. Being able to adapt is key to any business's survival.

Online print on demand merchandise, book royalties, meal delivery products, meal delivery services are just a few of the multiple streams of income that you can create to meet the most extreme business challenges.

Chapter 12
Million Dollar
Restaurant
Business Rolodex

Restaurant Business Rolodex

Restaurant Supplies & Equipment

Oven and ranges.

webstaurantstore.com/cooking-equipment.html

Basic cooking equipment.

webstaurantstore.com/cooking-equipment.html

Microwave ovens.

Amazon.com (microwave ovens commercial grade)

Convection ovens.

Restaurantsupply.com (convection ovens)

Fryers.

Resfab.com

Food preparation tables.

Mixwholesale.com

Restaurant Business Rolodex

Restaurant Supplies & Equipment

Merchandisers.

Chefscloset.com

faire.com

papermart.com

Sinks and faucets.

Katom.com

Ice machines and accessories.

wasserstrom.com

Transportation carts and racks.

globalindustrial.com

Shelving.

uline.com

Restaurant Business Rolodex

FINANCING

http://sbarestaurantloans.com/

http://www.restaurant-financing.com/

http://unitedcapitalsource.com/index-ppc.php?ref=MSN.com-MSN-Rest-(BM)-Restaurant-Financing&seed=Restaurant-Financing

SOFTWARE

http://freerestaurantsoftware.com/

http://www.restaurantsoftware.com/

http://restaurantfunds.com/

MARKETING

http://www.mplans.com/restaurant_marketing_plan/marketing_vision_fc.php

http://www.squidoo.com/HowToStartaRestaurantBusiness

Restaurant Business Rolodex

TRANSPORTATION

Used Trucks/CARS Online

https://gsaauctions.gov/gsaauctions/gsaauctions/

ebay.com/motors

uhaul.com/TruckSales/

https://ryder.com/used-trucks

penskeusedtrucks.com

Parts

http://www.truckchamp.com/

http://www.autopartswarehouse.com/

Restaurant Business Rolodex

TRANSPORTATION

Bikes & Motorcycles

http://gsaauctions.gov/gsaauctions/aucindx/

bikesdirect.com

http://www.bti-usa.com/

urbanscooters.com

COMPUTERS/Office Equipment

outletpc.com/

Restaurant Business Rolodex

Computer Tool Kits

dhgate.com

aliexpress.com

wholesalecomputercables.com

tigerdirect.com

Computer Parts

laptopuniverse.com

sabcal.com

other

nearbyexpress.com

commercialbargains.co

getpaid2workfromhome.com

boyerblog.com

Restaurant Business Rolodex

American merchandise liquidators

http://www.amlinc.com/

the closeout club

http://www.thecloseoutclub.com/

RJ discount sales

http://www.rjsks.com/

St louis wholesale

http://www.stlouiswholesale.com/

Wholesale Electronics

http://www.weisd.com/

http://www.anawholesale.com/

office wholesale

http://www.1-computerdesks.com/

1aaa wholesale merchandise

http://www.1aaawholesalemerchandise.com/

Restaurant Business Rolodex

big lots wholesale

http://www.biglotswholesale.com/

More Business Resources

1.   http://www.sba.gov/content/starting-green-business

home based businesses

2.   http://www.sba.gov/content/home-based-business

3.   online businesses

http://www.sba.gov/content/setting-online-business

4.   self employed and independent contractors

http://www.sba.gov/content/self-employed-independent-contractors

5.   minority owned businesses

http://www.sba.gov/content/minority-owned-businesses

6.   veteran owned businesses

http://www.sba.gov/content/veteran-service-disabled-veteran-owned

Restaurant Business Rolodex

7.   woman owned businesses

http://www.sba.gov/content/women-owned-businesses

8.   people with disabilities

http://www.sba.gov/content/people-with-disabilities

9.   young entrepreneurs

http://www.sba.gov/content/young-entrepreneurs

Chapter 13

Business Terms & Definitions

Business Terms & Definitions

Accounts – Companies produce a annual set of accounts. If you are listed on the stock exchange you have to give info on profits six months into the financial year.

Actuary – Actuaries work for insurance companies and pension providers and calculate life expectancy, accident rates and likely payouts by using math algorithms.

Business Plan – A business plan is a formal statement of business goals, reasons they are attainable, and plans for reaching them. It may also contain background information about the organization or team attempting to reach those goals.

Balance Sheet – a statement of the assets, liabilities, and capital of a business or other organization at a particular point in time, detailing, the balance of income and expenditure over the preceding period.

Business Terms & Definitions

Bear Market – A stock market in which share prices fall precipitously, typically 15%-20%.

Bull Market – A market when prices roar ahead.

Capital Gains – A capital gain refers to profit that results from a sale of a capital asset, such as stock, bond or real estate, where the sale price exceeds the purchase price. The gain is the difference between a higher selling price and a lower purchase price.

Capital Gains Tax – a tax levied on profit from the sale of property or of an investment.

Chapter 11 Bankruptcy – Chapter 11 is a chapter of Title 11 of the United States Bankruptcy Code, which permits reorganization under the bankruptcy laws of the United States. Chapter 11 bankruptcy is available to every business, whether organized as a corporation, partnership or sole proprietorship, and to individuals, although it is most prominently used by corporate entities.

Business Terms & Definitions

Consumers Prices Index – The Consumer Price Index (CPI) is a measure that examines the weighted average of prices of a basket of consumer goods and services, such as transportation, food and medical care. It is calculated by taking price changes for each item in the predetermined basket of goods and averaging them.

Day Trading - Day Trading is the buying and selling of stocks during the trading day buy punters on their own account. The aim is to make a profit on the day and have no open positions at the close of the trading session.

Dow Jones Industrial Average – The Dow Jones Industrial Average (DJIA) is a price-weighted average of 30 significant stocks traded on the New York Stock Exchange (NYSE) and the NASDAQ. The DJIA was invented by Charles Dow back in 1896.

Diminishing Returns – used to refer to a point at which the level of profits or benefits gained is less than the amount of money or energy invested.

Business Terms & Definitions

Economic Growth – Economic growth is the increase in the inflation adjusted market value of the goods and services produced by an economy over time. It is conventionally measured as the percent rate of increase in real gross domestic product or real GDP.

Equity – the value of the shares issued by a company.

Elasticity – elasticity is a measure of a variable's sensitivity to a change in another variable. In business and economics, elasticity refers the degree to which individuals, consumers or producers change their demand or the amount supplied in response to price or income changes.

Fiscal Year – The US fiscal year runs from October 1 to September 30.

Foreign Exchange (Forex) – Foreign exchange, or forex, markets are where one currency is exchanged for another.

Business Terms & Definitions

FORM 501 – A 501(c) organization is a nonprofit organization in the federal law of the United States according to 26 U.S.C. 501 and is one of 29 types of nonprofit organizations which are exempt from some federal income taxes.

Form 701 – General Information. Registration of a Limited Liability Partnership.

Grant – Grants are non-repayable funds or products disbursed or gifted by one party (grant makers), often a government department, corporation, foundation or trusts to a recipient, often (but not always) a nonprofit entity, educational institution, business or an individual.

Gross Domestic Product – GDP is the sum of all goods and services produced in the economy, including the service sector, manufacturing, construction, energy, agriculture and government.

Business Terms & Definitions

Gross National Product – the total value of goods produced and services provided by a country during one year, equal to the gross domestic product plus the net income from foreign investments.

Hedge Funds – a limited partnership of investors that uses high risk methods, such as investing with borrowed money, in hopes of realizing large capital gains.

Income Statement – An income statement is one of the financial statements of a company and shows the company's revenues and expenses during a particular period.

Income Tax – tax levied by a government directly on income, especially an annual tax on personal income.

Inheritance Tax – a tax imposed on someone who inherits property or money.

Business Terms & Definitions

Inflation – a general increase in prices and fall in the purchasing value of money.

Limited Liability Company (LLC) – A limited liability company (LLC) is a corporate structure whereby the members of the company cannot be held personally liable for the company's debts or liabilities. Limited liability companies are essentially hybrid entities that partnership or sole proprietorship.

Loan to Value – The loan-to-value (LTV) ratio is a financial term used by lenders to express the ratio of a loan to the value of an asset purchased. The term is commonly used by banks and building societies to represent the ration of the first mortgage line as a percentage of the total appraised value of real property.

Microloan – a small sum of money lent at low interest to a new business.

Business Terms & Definitions

Mutual Fund – an investment program funded by shareholders that trades in diversified holdings and is professionally managed.

NASDAQ – The National Association of Securities Dealers Automated Quotations (NASDAQ) was set up in 1971 as an international screen-based trading system without a central dealing floor. In 1998 it merged with the American Stock exchange (Amex).

Occupational Pension Scheme – Occupational pension schemes may be contributory or non-contributory, funded or unfunded, defined benefit or defined contribution. In contributory schemes, both you and your employer pay contributions towards the scheme. In non-contributory schemes, you do not contribute buy your employer does.

Partnership – A legal form of business operation between tow or more individuals who share management and profits. The federal government recognizes several types of partnerships. The two most common are general and limited partnerships. A limited partnership has both general and limited partners.

Business Terms & Definitions

Rate of Return – A rate of return is the gain or loss on an investment over a specified time period, expressed as a percentage of the investment's cost. Gains on investments are defined as income received plus any capital gains realized on the sale of the investment.

Real Estate Investment Trusts – A real estate investment trust (REIT) is a company that owns, and in most cases operates, income-producing real estate. REITs own many types of commercial real estate, ranging from office and apartment buildings to warehouses, shopping centers and hotels.

SBA - The Small Business Administration (SBA0 is a U.S. Government agency, formulated in 1953, that operates autonomously. This agency was established to bolster and promote the economy in general by providing assistance to small businesses.

Business Terms & Definitions

SCORE (SBA) – SCORE is a nonprofit organization that provides free business mentoring services to prospective and established small business owners in the United States. More than 10,000 volunteers provide these services, with all volunteers being active and retired business executives and entrepreneurs.

Sole Proprietorship – A business that legally has no separate existence from its owner. Income and losses are taxed on the individual's personal income tax return. The sole proprietorship is the simplest business form under which one can operate a business. The sole proprietorship is not a legal entity.

Tax Haven – Generic term for geographical area outside the jurisdiction of one's home country which imposes only a few restriction on legitimate business activities within its jurisdiction, and little or no income tax. Also called a low tax jurisdiction, non tax jurisdiction, or offshore haven.

Business Terms & Definitions

Value Added Tax – A value added tax (VAT) is a consumption tax added to a product's sales price. It represents a tax on the "value added" to the product throughout its production process.

Wall Street – Wall Street is a street in lower Manhattan that is the original home of the New York Stock Exchange and the historic headquarters of the largest U.S. Brokerages and investment banks.

Yield – The yield is the income return on an investment, such as the interest or dividends received from holding a particular security. The yield is usually expressed as an annual percentage rate based on the investment's cost, current market value or face value.

Zero Interest Rates – A zero interest rate policy is a route taken by a central bank to keep the base rate at zero percent in an attempt to stimulate demand in the economy by making the supply of money cheaper.